TI [illegible]

NATURE'S COSMIC PICTURE GALLERY

Theoosophical Manual No. 10

The Astral Light

Nature's Cosmic Picture Gallery

By

HENRY TRAVERS EDGE

POINT LOMA PUBLICATIONS, INC.
P.O. BOX 6507
SAN DIEGO, CALIFORNIA 92106

Third printing 1986

ISBN: 0913004-20-0

Printed in the United States of America by
Stockton Trade Press, Inc.
Buena Park, California

CONTENTS

EDITORS' PREFACE

Nature exists and Man exists, and somewhere, unobscured by man's own sophistries there must be available the wisdom and learning which tells us *why* and *how*. As we ponder the question it seems an inevitable conclusion that somewhere there must be preserved a recording, a gathering of facts or 'laws', a formulation in human language of the truth concerning Man and Nature. There must be a basic source from which sciences, philosophies and great religions have sprung.

H. P. Blavatsky, in her writings of immense intellectual and spiritual power — still not fully appreciated — points to that living Source, declaring it exists. She called it the Ancient Wisdom, the Sacred Science, the *Gupta-Vidyâ,* and gave to it the Greek name of *Theosophia,* Theosophy, knowledge and wisdom such as the gods or divinities live by. This Ancient Wisdom, she affirmed, has always been in existence, though not always publicly known, having come down the ages tested and checked by generations of Great Seers. It may be called the Facts of Being, the 'laws' or workings of Nature.

In this series of twelve Theosophical Manuals this Ancient Wisdom in its fundamentals is explained with clarity of presentation and logical appeal by students and scholars who have devoted a lifetime to theosophic study. Above all they have been governed by strict honesty and adherence to the teachings as originally reported and recorded.

The first booklet, *Theosophy: A General View of Occult Doctrine,* outlines the overall teachings, presenting a general picture. Succeeding booklets cover in greater detail the subjects of Reincarnation, Karma, The Seven Principles of Man, Death and the After-Death States of Consciousness, Evolution, Man's Divine Parentage: the Origin of Man and of the Earth, the Doctrine of Cycles, The Ladder of Life: Hierarchies, The Astral Light, Psychic Powers, and Theosophy and Christianity.

It is hoped that these Studies will be received with an open mind, for in them the earnest searcher will find keys that are indispensable to an understanding of the Universe and of Man.

Helen Todd
W. Emmett Small

I

INTRODUCTORY

THE work of Theosophists and of various cults which have originated in that work have familiarized us with the word 'astral' in such expressions as 'astral body,' 'seeing in the astral light,' 'getting on to the astral plane'; and in the following pages an attempt is made to furnish inquirers with an outline of the subject in accordance with the Theosophical teachings. The entire subject is vast and comprehensive; but, as with other subjects, it is possible to begin with what may be called an elementary text-book, which shall outline the main features without perplexing the neophyte with too many details, leaving these latter to be mastered in the course of further studies of the Theosophical teachings.

Though much has been written about the astral light in other works, we have in mind in this manual a particular object, and that is to relate the subject to the most recent changes in world-thought which have taken place, especially as regards the scientific outlook. In a world in which the old-fashioned scientific universe is regarded as a plenum, and in which Nature and her laws are held to be fully explained by scientific formulas, such a conception as the astral light may appear to belong to that mysterious category known as the 'supernatural.' Here however the supernatural will be entirely rejected, and we propose to show that the astral light is a part of Nature, and an *essential* part of Nature. It is realized today by men of science themselves that their former conceptions are by no means adequate to an explanation of the natural phenomena which have now come under their ken; and they are actually feeling their way towards ideas comfortable to the Theosophical teachings.

The restricted spheres of both religion and science have left unexplored a very large realm of Nature and of human experience, thus leaving us without guidance in a realm which it is of the utmost importance for us to understand. This lack is partially and very inadequately filled by various schools of psychology, psycho-analysis, and the like, which are groping largely in the dark. Again there is the whole vast subject of the 'Night Side of Nature'—apparitions, wraiths, presentiments, haunted houses, and the like, the reality of which is so well attested that few remain today who feel able to get away with a simple denial of the facts. Such things are natural, a part of nature, and demand to be explained and understood.

II

MEANING OF THE TERM 'ASTRAL LIGHT'

THIS term, though perhaps not the best that could be chosen, has come down to us from certain medieval mystics and passed into current use. 'Astral' means starry, and was used both by ancient and medieval philosophers to designate spheres above the terrestrial or earthy. In the same way such spheres were often spoken of as spheres of light, or fire, or aether. As to the word 'light,' we might substitute the word 'matter' and speak of astral matter instead of astral light. But in this case it would be a kind of matter that was self-luminous. We might also speak of the astral plane; and this may help us to realize that we need to feel more certain as to just what such words as 'light,' 'matter,' 'plane,' really mean. How does science regard light? If it is a vibration, then we must suppose some vibrating medium, and this medium must be of a material nature. And if light is not vibration, then we must suppose that it is itself a form of matter.

Theosophy recognizes several different

planes of Nature. The plane familiar to us is called the physical plane; it is related to our physical senses. These senses are limited in their scope; they give us a partial view of Nature. While they are commonly regarded as our means of communication with Nature, it is also possible to regard them as windows which only allow us to see a small part of Nature and shut us out from the rest. From the reports received from these senses we have constructed an imaginary picture of the universe: put in technical language, we have a set of concepts derived from our percepts. If we have other senses, more subtle ones, and these should come into play while our former senses became inactive, we should get quite another picture of the universe. Things which we have taken for granted, because we are so familiar with them, and which we have assumed to be universal and invariable, would be seen to be peculiar to the physical plane, to our physical consciousness, and not necessarily appropriate to other planes. Notions of space and time and magnitude and position and density and force might be entirely different. We should have left the physical plane; we should be on the astral plane, in the astral light.

It is often convenient to consider the universe under threefold aspects, just as we may consider man as spirit-soul-body. In this view the astral light would be the intermediate sphere between the spiritual and the physical, and thus it would be the soul of the world — as indeed it has often been called. Thus the Astral Light, in this view, would form a connecting link between the higher and lower worlds; it would stand to the higher world in the relation of a body, and to the lower world in the relation of a spirit. But it must be pointed out that such a three-fold division of the universe is not a complete analysis, and is only adopted for the convenience of a concise view; for Theosophy divides the universe into many planes. In this latter view the Astral Light is the plane immediately above the physical plane, and is the lowest of a number of cosmic planes, reaching from the physical plane to the highest spiritual plane, in a gradation of steps of greater and greater refinement. To these other planes various names are given such as Âkâśa and Aether; but it is not necessary at present to go into details as to these distinctions.

Thus the Astral Light or Astral Plane is another world, or another story of the world, related to a different set of senses in man, and characterized by different relations of space, time, and other qualities. If it be asked whether the Astral Light is a form of matter or a form of energy, it may be answered that the former distinction made between these two by science is now becoming obliterated, and it is coming to be recognized that there is no essential distinction between matter and energy. Both of them are now regarded as particular and contrasted phases or aspects of some one thing which is more fundamental than either. What to call this one thing, and how to define it is a question that now engages the attention of of physicists. It is a very old idea that there must exist a permanent substratum to Nature, a basic substance, a protyle, an 'absolute,' a *prima materia,* of which all the various elements known to science are merely modifications; and not only so, but all the various forms of energy are also modifications. The quest for such a basic substance is one form of the quest for the 'philosopher's stone,' the great magic agent.

III

SCIENTIFIC VIEWS

PHYSICAL science has found itself involved in difficulties and contradictions by the attempt to explain all physical phenomena in terms of physics alone; and has presented us with a picture of a universe composed of indestructible units of matter, acted on by forces. But, if these forces are material themselves, we have matter impelling matter; and if they are not material, they must be something else — say spiritual — and materialistic science did not recognize any such thing. Further, this scheme does not provide any means of explaining how the immaterial forces can act on the material forces, or (which is the same thing) how energy can act across spaces assumed to be empty. These and similar difficulties disappear at once, as soon as we regard the physical world as merely a manifestation of energies acting behind the scenes, so that we can see the effects but not the causes, the shifting scenes but not the sceneshifters. We may now say, with all the authority of modern science behind us, that the former supposed permanent and indivisible atom of matter has now become resolved into a mere center of vibrations and energies; and this makes it necessary to assume a subtler and ultra-physical form of matter in which these vibrations and energies can inhere. Thus we have full authority for presuming the reality of at least one grade of matter which is not physical matter, and whose properties must therefore be different from those of physical matter. Also we can say that this matter partakes in an equal degree of the qualities usually assigned to energy and force. It becomes desirable therefore to use some such expression as 'force-substance' or 'energy-matter,' to designate such an entity which is neither the one nor the other but both.

In view of the above, we can scarcely be accused of fantasy when we speak of the Astral Light as a world of energy-substance of a subtler order than the physical world, and underlying the latter as its prime mover.

The physical world, as compared with the astral world, is a world of results; while the astral world is to the physical world as a world of causes. The astral world is a world of forms and types, which find their expression in the physical world. This idea is necessary in order to account for many quite familiar happenings, which have no real explanation on orthodox lines of the older physics. Take for example the production of a tree from a seed. It may be granted that the materials for the tree are gathered from the soil and the atmosphere; but that is not enough explanation; we require to know why each seed should produce a tree comformable to its own nature and build these materials into one particular pattern and no other. It is because the entire pattern of the future tree is contained within the seed, and the growth of that seed is simply a process of unfoldment, during which the particles from soil and air are gathered together and built into the required form. And let us bear in mind that no question of size, no question of how such a large pattern can be packed into such a small seed, is relevant; for it has already been shown that our physical notions of space and dimension do not necessarily, or even probably, apply to the astral world. If thought desirable, we might here invoke that old friend the 'fourth dimension' as a possible means of escape from the difficulty.

We can easily extend our illustration of the seed and tree to other familiar cases. For instance, what explanation can physics give for the way in which the human body preserves its integrity of shape, although its physical particles are continually changing, some being cast off, others taken on? Why does a mole persists in the same place throughout life? If we try to evade the point by saying that the new particles take the same *place* as the old particles, then it is legitimate to inquire, What is a *place?* And it will be a puzzle to define a place apart from any objects which may occupy it. The rational explanation is that there is an astral body within the physical body, and that this inner body remains unchanged throughout all the changes of physical substance.

This is a topic which belongs more particularly to discussions on the constitution of man, and to the astral body in man;* to which the reader may be referred; but it is impossible to avoid overlapping, so intimately are the various Theosophical teachings interblended. In the same way we might adduce the phenomena of memory, a faculty which enables us to preserve the image of events, despite the continual changes in the physical substance of the brain. But we must deal specifically with the Astral Light in Nature, rather than as manifested in man particularly.

---

*Manual No. IV, *Man and his Seven Principles,* by L. L. Wright.

IV

A COSMIC PICTURE GALLERY

THE Astral Light has been well called the world's memory and the cosmic picture gallery. It is Nature's storehouse of forms. Everything in the physical world pre-exists in the astral world as an image or type or form. Besides this, it is a great memory, Nature's memory; for it retains impressions of objects and events on the physical plane. Thus it is a great record. The thoughts of men perish not when the thinker dies; they have passed out into the astral light; where their records remain, and whence they can be recovered by the vision of the trained seer. This suggests that nothing can ever be irrecoverably lost. This carries us beyond the familiar notion of the passage of time, and offers us a picture in which past, present, and future coexist as one whole. The astral light contains the germs of all that is to be on the physical plane, and the records of all that has been.

Here again the recent advances in scientific philosophy will help us to an understanding. In seeking to interpret the more recent findings of experimental research, it has been found no longer sufficient to regard merely the position which objects occupy in space; it becomes necessary to define their position in *time*. And thus a fourth co-ordinate is added to the familiar spatial three, and we not only ask *where* a thing is, but *when*. And in place of objects we speak of *events*. With this help it becomes easier to understand how the astral light may be a storehouse of events.

Many familiar phenomena have been pushed aside or declared impossible for no better reason than that they could not be explained by the orthodox science of the time. But when we have a simple explanation ready to hand there is no reason to reject them or to try not to see them. Thought transference is a matter of common occurrence, especially between people closely related or associated with each other. We often fail to remember something and leave off trying; and later on the memory comes back unexpectedly. We fail to solve a problem, and the solution pops into our head suddenly at some later time. We live in an atmosphere of thought, just as we live in an atmosphere of air; and ideas come into the head from we know not where, and pass out again we know not whither. Thoughts are things; they may not come under the definition of physical matter as 'that which can be handled and weighed'; but we have seen that there may be other sorts of matter, having altogether different properties.

It is not only thoughts, but also emotions, which are stored up in the astral light and passed from one human being to another; and this explains the unconscious and unseen influence which we exercise upon one another. It is really impossible to sin in secret; an evil thought or feeling will poison the astral light as a dirty body would foul the water in which we bathed, or an unwholesome breath might pollute the atmosphere. On the other side of the picture, our good thoughts and aspirations must have their influence; and this influence is more potent because it rises to a higher plane. The importance of individual responsibility becomes greatly increased in view of this. And this leads us to speak of the connection of the astral light with the law of Karma.

V

THE ASTRAL LIGHT AND KARMA

WHILE we may believe that our present experiences are the fruit of our past acts or thoughts, and that our present acts and thoughts will beget future consequences for ourselves, we often fail to see the links connecting cause with effect. This is not surprising in view of the limitation of our knowledge of Nature: we see only a small part of Nature, and there must be much that we do not see. But the teaching about the astral light will enable us to supply some of the missing links. Every act, every thought and desire, imprints itself on the astral light, so that man may be said to 'people his current in space' with his own creations, the offspring of his thoughts and deeds. And the consequences of such acts will return to their doer in accordance with two laws, for which we readily find analogies in physical science. One is the law of action and reaction; the other is the law that like attracts like. Any energy thrown forth in one direction tends, when the force is spent, to flow back in the opposite direction, as in the swing of a pendulum or a stone that is tossed up; and as each impression is stamped with the quality of its creator, the law of affinity tends to bring it back to him. Karma is the adjuster of disturbed equilibrium; it may even be said that what we call an act is only half an act; the whole act includes the reaction as well. But the deed and its reaction may be separated by long intervals, so that we fail to trace the connection. The two may even be separated by the gap of physical death, so that the causes set in motion in one incarnation will not yield their results until a later incarnation. But the astral light provides for this; for it is the great storehouse of Nature and can preserve impressions indefinitely.

Misunderstanding as to karma may be caused by confusing physical acts with moral acts; and much of this misunderstanding will be cleared up if we bear in mind that the astral light is only one of seven cosmic planes, and that karma acts on all planes. Also, we must remember that karma is not a blind mechanism, such as is imagined by materialistic thought. There can be no such thing as a blind mechanism anywhere; life and consciousness lie behind all phenomena, even the phenomena of physical matter, as is better realized now than it was last century. It may be convenient sometimes to use mechanical terms in speaking of karma and the astral light, but we must not forget that the astral light, like the rest of Nature, is alive. Spirit and matter are opposite poles of the same fundamental substance; and the higher we advance from physical matter up through the various cosmic planes towards spirit, the more accentuated become the spiritual qualities. So the astral light may be thought of as an intermediate grade between spirit and matter, or between mind and matter (it is hard to find exact terms in our language) ; and when we remember that there are seven planes of the astral light, we can more readily understand how mind and matter may be connected by a series of graduating links.

When we speak of a chain of causation connecting acts with their results, we must bear in mind that the links in this chain are not the inert bodies dealt with in physical mechanics, but are more or less conscious living beings, endowed with volition and purpose to a greater or less extent. It is taught that when a thought-form leaves our mind it may coalesce with an *elemental,* and by this coalescence there is engendered a living being, which thereupon begins a life of its own. Its conscious life consists entirely in the tendency to repeat the act which it represents, so that it is instinctual and is not endowed with more intelligence than is necessary to enable it to execute that function. Here then we have an intelligible explanation of the phenomenon called 'habit,' as also of a large class of actions known as impulsive. Each one of us has surrounded himself with a host of such elemental beings, which are continually trying to express themselves through our minds or our bodily mechanism. Such words as 'tendency,' 'proclivity,' and the like, as used in common parlance or by science, are mere counters; they are abstract nouns or uncashed checks or algebraic letters for unknown values; so that our explanation is not superfluous but necessary.

As soon as we begin to study our own daily experiences, with the above ideas in mind, we shall find plenty of corroboration for the teachings. Previously we had overlooked this evidence, because we were not seeking it. It helps people greatly in the work of understanding and ruling themselves, if they can realize that they are to a great extent permitting themselves to be controlled by actual obsessing beings—namely, these thought-elementals and elementals of desire, continually prompting to unconsidered speech or acts, and inspiring moods of anger, sarcasm, levity, etc., which we afterwards regret; and a poor excuse it is to say that 'I don't know what made me do it, but something came over me.'

VI

DANGERS OF THE LOWER ASTRAL LIGHT

THAT stratum of the astral light which lies nearest to the physical earth is its lowest and coarsest layer; and it is this layer which teems with what might be called the effluvia of men's thoughts and emotions and passions and gross actions. This region is peopled with a great variety of beings, endowed with little or no intelligence, instinctual in their action, for the most part harmful to men; and there is constant interaction between the two planes. For the most of us, our physical bodies act as a merciful shield, shutting us out from these influences and protecting us against their noxious influence. The Theosophical teachings tell us that, after the death of the body, a ghost survives for a time in the astral realms, awaiting what is called the 'second death,' which liberates the soul from its astral remnants. The extensive lore of ghost stories, apparitions, warnings, banned spirits, hauntings, etc., provides abundant evidence of the actuality of this belief, which has been familiar to humankind in all ages and countries. In cases where the person has died with a strong desire in his mind, his double has appeared to survivors, seeking their prayers or the burial of its bones, and so forth. The astral remains of very sensual and evil persons survive in the astral light, and seek to perpetuate their existence by preying upon the living; and this accounts for many cases of what can only be described as obsession. We often read in the papers of comparatively harmless but nervously unstable individuals being seized with sudden unaccountable homicidal mania, and perpetrating some act of violence which they afterwards regret and are unable to account for.

In short, not to dwell on a topic treated elsewhere in our literature, we may describe this lower astral light as a most undesirable region tenanted by a variety of undesirable beings. Those therefore who presumptuously seek to force an entry into this realm are guilty of a most unwise action; they may open a door which they cannot shut again; they may establish links which they cannot again sever; they may expose themselves to temptations which they cannot resist; they may upset the delicate balance of their nervous system and their mental and emotional nature. To engage in any practices with a view to opening up communication with the astral plane or its denizens, is conduct which can only be described as the foolhardiness of ignorance carried to a high degree. Only an exceptionally strong, pure, and trained character can withstand the dangers of this realm; and it is not without justification that students of Occultism are warned against any such procedure.

VII

THE ASTRAL LIGHT AND EVOLUTION

THIS is a topic which is treated in the Manual *Evolution** and perhaps elsewhere, but a few words thereon will be appropriate here. Science has found difficulty in making facts fit theories, because it regards the physical world only. The physical organisms of plants and animals present a series of graduated forms, and their resemblances give rise to the idea that they are derived, the one from the other, by a process called biological evolution. But observation has proved that these species are a set of disconnected links, each remaining true to its own kind, and with no visible connecting links or gradations between them. It is even found that variations produced by an alteration of the environment, such as happens when we cultivate domestic breeds, are not permanent, but that there is a tendency for the species to revert to its original type as soon as the special environment is removed. This difficulty arises from

*No. VI of this series.

not taking into account the astral plane. The changes by which one type passes into another take place in the astral form, which is plastic.

Actually the organism is a living, conscious soul, which grows, develops, and changes by its own evolutionary purpose; these changes are then transmitted to the astral form, and thence to the physical organism. But it is only when the change has been completed astrally that its physical counterpart appears. Thus the physical organisms do not present an unbroken continuous line, but a succession of steps. When we view a spiral staircase from one side, we see a number of separate stages, one above another, but do not see the continuous stairway by which these are connected.

VIII

THE ASTRAL LIGHT AND ETHER

ACCORDING to the atomo-mechanical theory of the universe, we have atoms separated from each other by empty spaces, and yet acting on each other; and the difficulty has been to provide an explanation for this seeming action at a distance. It would seem that it is necessary to suppose a medium between the atoms, for the conveyance of energy from one to another. If this medium is itself material, we have not solved the original problem, but merely moved it one step farther. But if the medium is not material, what is it? Again, in order to supplement the undulatory theory of light, it was necessary to suppose a medium, purely hypothetical and not subject to direct observation, to which was given the name of *ether*. Many obstacles were encountered because theorists would insist on trying to endow this ether with the properties of physical matter, especially as to density and rigidity. But all that was really necessary in this medium was that it should be able to transmit vibrations, and there was no justification for attributing to it those other properties which are associated with vibration in physical matter. It is clear that what is needed is a form of ultra-physical matter; and its properties can only be ascertained by experiment, and not by inference and calculation from known physical data. There must be a substratum for the manifestation of luminous, electro-magnetic, and cosmic ray phenomena; and this would seem to answer to one of the subdivisions of the astral light. The astral light, instead of being an annex or upper story to nature, is a necessary component, and without it the physical universe would fall apart or be reduced to absolute stagnation.

Such things as weather, storms, and earthquakes, also stand in need of the astral light to complete the explanation. Science may assign meteorological phenomena to a number of secondary causes, such as convection currents in the atmosphere, deflected by the earth's rotation; and they may trace them farther back to magnetic conditions, and even to fluctuations in the magnetic field caused by what goes on upon the sun. A knowledge of the astral light enables us to carry the chain of causation a step farther. Moreover it supplies a link between the mental and moral atmosphere of mankind and the terrestrial phenomena which are so often suspected of being related to them. Earthquakes are attended by various mechanical phenomena, such as subsidences and the slipping of faults; but it is at least an open question whether these should be regarded as causes or as effects. Besides, it is well known that most animals and some human being can feel the approach of an earthquake before it happens. If the earth is a vast globe, subject to continual contraction through loss of heat, the great wonder is that it remains as still as it does; and we wonder if it is not perhaps *held* still. The Theosophical teaching is that the astral light is subject to tensions, caused by the thoughts and emotions of mankind; and that such tensions find sudden relief, thus agitating the crust of the earth. As to meteorological phenomena in general, it is obvious that, however many physical causes we may assign to them, they are still left in the category of 'chance;' but, when we introduce the astral light as a factor, we see a way of connecting these happenings with the mental and moral condition of the inhabitants of the earth; the unsatisfactory idea of chance is avoided, and rationality is introduced into the explanation. Earthquakes occur most frequently in particular regions, but it is natural that when anything is shaken it should give way in its weakest spots, where the rocks are displaced or broken or where there is a dynamical tension due to inequality of pressure. There should nowadays be enough machinery at the disposal of science, in the way of sunspots and electromagnetic influence, to carry the explanation of earthquakes a step farther than mere mechanism; but still there would be a lack of links to connect them with mental and moral phenomena.

IX

THE ASTRAL LIGHT AND HISTORY

WE HAVE spoken of the need for the astral light in order to give a scientific explanation of Nature, of the impossibility of explaining evolution without it, and of its rôle in showing the connection between man's acts and the results which he reaps from them. We have now to show how necessary the idea is for a rational understanding of history. In history, as elsewhere, the current views may be roughly divided into the theistic and the rationalistic. According to the former it is Providence which directs events; the latter seeks to represent history as a causal chain in which past events determine future events, or as a kind of evolution. It is very evident that, if history were such a chain of cause and effect, with no influence entering it from without, it would resemble a stream slowly winding down hill, and could not possibly rise to any higher source. The Providence idea is much the better of the two; without Providence we must fain introduce vague unknown influences grouped under the word 'chance,' a word which is merely a confession of ignorance.

History is the complex drama of human souls, each one growing and evolving, and all interacting with one another, the whole movement being fed by a continual fount of inspiration from within each individual. And the most potent effects are seen to be produced by a comparatively few individuals of extraordinary power, who give birth to new ideas, initiate movements, inaugurate new eras of thought, becoming the center of groups and passing on their work to their followers. But what we are considering in this place is the function of the astral light in the historical process. Thoughts mold events, but the astral light is the medium between thoughts and events. Hence the action of thoughts on events is not immediate and direct. The astral light acts as a great storer and accumulator, receiving impress from thoughts, and gradually transmitting that impress to events. As each individual man bears about with him his character in the form of habits impressed upon his own astral substance by his past thoughts and acts, so on the large scale there are national characters and racial characters, due to deep impressions in the astral light; and these may be called habits on the large scale. The tremendous force and fixity of such habits, or fashions, or prejudices, or racial characters, is well known. In what do they inhere? What answer can science give? The intimate biological study of heredity has given us a notion of germ-cells handed on from generation to generation, whose function it is to preserve the type amid temporary variations.

Here then we have a ghost of an explanation; but the germ-cell is a very small apex upon which to balance so great a weight; at best it is a detail in the process. These tendencies inhere in nature's great storehouse, the astral light. It surrounds the earth like a mighty atmosphere in which we all live. Each race and nation has its own astral light, and the whole of humanity has its astral light. This stores up impressions tenaciously and enduringly, and it takes a great deal to change them. How else explain the well-nigh indelible characteristics of nations, lasting through the centuries and handed on with every succeeding generation? We are all born into such a ready-made atmosphere, and it takes a strong individual character to contend against it and modify its influence.

Many unaccountable happenings in history find ready explanation in this way. Take for instance the famous gunpowder plot in the reign of James I of England. Historians are at a loss to explain why a group of gentlemen of excellent character should incontinently decide to blow up the king, the royal family, and the whole of the House of Lords, House of Commons, and various government executives in one vast massacre, which would have left the nation at the mercy of mob law and might well have brought the separate national existence of England to an end; and should have actually placed the powder and stationed the desperado with his matches, only to be thwarted at the last moment by what seemed a mere accident. What influence could make people depart so far from their natural character as to commit an atrocity of such unparalleled magnitude? The answer is found in the state of the human mind in those times. Europe was mad over religious controversies; France was split into rival creeds, bent on mutual extermination; the massacre of St. Bartholomew was recent. The infection had spread to England. It was what we should, in the jargon of today, call a psychic wave.

From time to time the astral light grows surcharged with influences from the thoughts of men; and as nature tends ever to restore equilibrium, relief is found in violent outbursts or psychic cataclysms, which are strictly analogous to epidemics of disease. The immediate consequences are disturbing, but the result is purification.

X

DENIZENS OF THE ASTRAL LIGHT

IT IS not to be supposed that there is any world, any plane of great Nature, not inhabited and peopled with living beings, even as is our own familiar physical plane. The whole universe teems with living beings, appropriate to their particular spheres. If men such as we could not live on the planets, this is no reason for inferring that there are no men at all there; and the same with the other planes of Nature. As physical beings live on the physical plane, so astral beings live on the astral plane, adapted to their habitat as we are to ours. It must however be confessed that this is a ticklish subject to deal with, and one of which it may be said with some truth that ignorance is bliss. For, as has been said, man is mercifully protected by his physical body from too close contact with the pernicious influences of the lower astral light, and to remove that protection prematurely is to court disaster.

Yet on the other hand knowledge may protect; so we must try to hold a just balance between these opposite maxims. To direct people's attention to pernicious astral denizens may be equivalent to encouraging them in the very thing they ought to avoid; for the morbid imagination of weak people may conjure up hobgoblins that have no existence outside that imagination, and cases of obsession are much better cured by a diversion of attention to healthy pursuits than by a morbid introspection or psycho-analysis of the slums of consciousness. Nevertheless it is of benefit to know that many of the impulses which we dignify by attributing them to ourselves may be actually the result of evil promptings from entities which are not ourselves at all but merely intrusive elements. It will place us on our guard and enable us to defeat them by taking our stand firmly on our own selfhood.

It is stated in the Manual *After Death—What?** that following the disintegration of the physical body of man there is a temporary survival of the astral and lower psychic parts of his constitution; and that in some cases this may persist for a long while, perpetuating its life by vampirizing the living; such contact being caused by weakness and intemperance in the living, or perhaps inadvertently courted through spiritualistic practices or dabbling in 'psychism.' Such a psychic remnant or 'spook' is of course destitute of the moral element, because all the

*No. V of this series.

higher part of the man's nature has separated and passed elsewhere; so that it is merely actuated by the desire to satisfy its gross instincts. So here is one kind of denizen of the lower astral light. The existence of earth-bound spirits, ghosts, larvae, etc., has always been recognized, and the mind will recall instances of various modes of worshiping them or propitiating them, or warding them off. Intercourse with such creatures is harmful both to them and to us, for they should be allowed to die out naturally and not kept in an unnatural existence.

Next we may consider that class of beings known by such names as Elementals, Fairies, Nature-Spirits, Nymphs, etc., etc. It is found that classical antiquity believed in nymphs, dryads, and other beings inhabiting rivers, mountains, forests, trees, etc.; and that many peoples of today whom we call uncivilized believe in such beings; also that there is no nation but has its stories of fairies and nature-spirits. This kind of belief is called by our wise men 'animism,' and defined as the practice of attributing life to non-living things. But these wiseacres have put the cart before the horse. It is they who have attributed inanimation to living things. The ancient and popular view is right. Everything in the universe is a living being of one kind or another. To the ancients a tree was a living soul, which they called a dryad or some similar name; the visible tree was merely the outer garment of this living being. The dryad did not inhabit the tree, but *was* the tree.

So with other nature-spirits; the astral light is the home of these beings, all of whom are on the path of evolution, each in its appropriate stage; it would be absurd to limit the number of kinds of animate beings to those alone who happen to be on the plane of physical matter. But this is a large subject and we must leave its special treatment for another occasion.

As for elementals, no physical action can take place without them; they constitute a necessary factor among those components which contribute to the performance of an action, and are represented in science by gaps which have to be provisionally filled by words of vague meaning, like 'force' or 'affinity.' What after all do we mean by the *properties* of matter? A more suitable expression would be the *dispositions, instincts,* or *proclivities* of matter. For mind lies behind all, and physical phenomena are merely the expression of mental states. Hence there must be in the astral world the elementals of all actions in the physical world. When we hum a tune we create an elemental, which is quite apt to worry us by insisting on being sung at inappropriate moments; as though we were haunted by a fly settling on us.

This little illustration will suggest fruitful thought as to the nature of habits; our actions generate elementals, endowed with our own vitality and tending to come again to repeat themselves and to be revitalized. Thus we get an idea of an elemental as a being which can only do one thing, and whose whole life consists in doing that thing over and over again. If this is not a good explanation of habits, we should always be ready to hear of better.

XI

SOCIAL INFLUENCE OF THE ASTRAL LIGHT

SINCE the astral light teems with influences put there by the thoughts and emotions of man, and since there is constant reaction of the astral light upon man, then it follows that the astral light must play a very important part in determining the conduct of man considered as a society. The appearance of epidemics of disease simultaneously in widely separated regions is but imperfectly accounted for by the theory of minute germs transported by people or blown on high air currents. And even so, we have still to explain the *origin* of such epidemics, whose incidence is so little connected with physical events and so unpredictable that we can only fall back upon such weak words as 'chance' and 'casual.' But, as has been said, physical events are the copy of astral events; physical epidemics follow upon astral epidemics, and these latter again are engendered by distempers in human thought. A familir analogy is provided by physical science. We cannot transmit a sound wave through the air from Europe to America, but we can transform that sound wave into etheric waves, then transmit them, and then reconvert them into sound waves. Similarly epidemics may be transmitted, and their transmission explained by regarding them as being conveyed on astral currents and reproduced as physical diseases elsewhere.

But apart from physical epidemics there are astral epidemics, or perhaps we should say psychic epidemics; and in the case of these also the usual physical explanations do not suffice to explain all the facts. The propagation of such epidemics is of course greatly increased by word of mouth and the influence of the press, but these material means will not explain all the phenomena; for we find waves of opinion, emotion, enthusiasm, sudden crazes, appearing without assignable cause in widely separated places at the same time.

History furnishes us with strange instances of epidemic hysterias, and in the present day we may find great religious revivals sweeping over countries, or a war fever spreading over the world. What is called 'crowd psychology' is well known and shows the existence of something which is much more than the mere sum-total of the minds of the component individuals; for these individuals are swept away against their own judgment. Such ideas should not be strange in view of the machinery now provided by science, in the shape of etheric waves, sun spots, etc., to explain the transmission of influences.

It has been said that 'Thoughts are Things,' and it is true. Ideas float into our mind, and we cannot tell where they come from; we work them over in our mind, and they pass from us, we know not whither. Of course there is a constant interchange of thoughts between people, and thought-forms are passing on currents in the astral light, like objects floating in water; we suck them in, and pass them out again in modified form. And not merely thoughts, but emotions—or, better still, thought-emotions; currents of energy which cause emotions in us and prompt to action. Which of us can claim to be master of his thoughts and emotions, immune against influences coming from an unseen source, able to stand independent of this general atmosphere in which we are immersed? Truly, our individual separation grows thin when we think of this thought-atmosphere which we all share, from which we receive, and to which we give. And think of the responsibility which is on each one of us! No man can sin alone; the privacy of his thoughts cannot shield him from guilt. A thought is an act, and every act produces consequences. Before blaming others for acts which we would not commit, do we not need to be sure of our own unexpressed desires and imagination? May we not ourselves have contributed to their delinquency?

But for consolation we may look at the other side of the picture and realize, as we have said before, that no *good* thought, no high aspiration, no feeling of true generous love and compassion, can be entertained by us without passing out from us as a potent force to work healing in other lives; and such a thought is all the more potent because it acts on a higher plane.

There are many problems studied by men of science and by those interested in bettering social conditions, which would be greatly clarified by an acquaintance with the astral light and with its counterpart the astral body of man. For instance, the question of heredity, which is by no means fully elucidated by the findings of scientific research. The microscope has revealed a number of minute factors, whose behavior has been most carefully studied; yet it is found that that behavior is unexpected and incalculable; so that what is studied is effects rather than causes. We see the scenes shifting but not those who stand behind and shift the scenery to and fro. It is just here that the Theosophical explanation steps in and completes that given by science. Logic could suggest that the causes of physical phenomena cannot themselves be physical; and, this being the case, it is useless to seek them in the physical world. What we can see under the microscope are things at the first stage of their appearance in physical three-dimensional space, and which previously have existed in the astral space. In this condition they do not come within the ken of the physical senses.

Heredity is by no means exclusively physical; it is also psychic and mental (not to mention other kinds); and the growing organism, both before and after birth, is subject to influence from the astral plane, which must yield effects that cannot be traced by a mere examination of the miscroscopic physiological processes. Such a science as eugenics, admirable though its aims may be, is handicapped by a too exclusive attention to the physical aspect of the question, and treating the problem as though it were the same for man as for animals. If this analogy holds good at all, then such a selective process of mating as is contemplated might be expected to produce a race excellent in physical and animal qualities, but lacking in most of what makes the man different from the animal. Legal restrictions on the multiplication of insane or degenerate types is one thing, and attempts to breed a superior race by scientific and legislative action is quite another. We need first to understand better the complex nature of man.

But this is not the place to multiply instances of this kind; and they may be left to the reader to supply for himself.

XII

PSYCHIC PHENOMENA, APPARITIONS, ETC.

SUBJECT to what has been said above about the great risks attending heedless dabbling in psychism, a word may be said as to the relation of the astral light to the above matters. There are innumerable accounts of apparitions of recently deceased persons, the foreseeing of coming calamities, ghostly warnings, the *poltergeist* or racketing spirit, and suchlike; and in these cases certain peculiar and comparatively infrequent conditions bring about a temporary connection between the astral and physical worlds. Relations of time, space, physical obstacles, etc., are seen to be different on the astral plane; communication between the living and the dead is difficult, and is often only achieved by the mediation of particular people endowed with a mediumistic constitution. A study of such records will provide much information and serve to confirm what we have said about the astral plane.

Glass, crystal, water, some metals, have a power of condensing (if that is the right word) the astral fluid, thus assisting the efforts of a seer; whence is explained the use of crystal globes, magic mirrors and the like. The phenomena of psychometry, by which some people are able, by handling some object such as a letter or article of attire, to arrive at much information about the writer or wearer, is an instance of the power which the astral light has of preserving images of events. It is an intriguing thought that nothing can perish; for psychometry proves to us by unimpeachable evidence that even scenes belonging to a remote past can thus be recovered. Explanations along the lines of our physical experience are out of order and are necessarily futile. Observation must precede theory; a large range of unfamiliar phenomena must be studied before we can venture to attempt their formulation into a set of laws.

Foreknowledge, prediction, the seeing of events not yet enacted in the physical world, presents a great obstacle to our power of conception. It is evident that here we have to deal with the nature of *time*. Coming events cast their shadow before them, it is said; if we can see the shadow, we may forecast the coming event. But what is foreseen is not a certainty; it is only a probability of greater or less degree. Some of the stories of forewarnings show that the foreseen danger was averted by the precautions taken by the dreamer or seer. It would seem that the astral time and physical time do not exactly gear together.

XIII

CONCLUDING REMARKS

STUDENTS of Theosophy, especially those new to the subject, may find themselves perplexed in seeking a definite idea of the relation of the astral light to other cosmic principles. There are several reasons for this. In the first place let it be said that it is not desirable to expect a too narrow and hard-and-fast definition, for by striving to do that we narrow down the idea into something which will fit conveniently into our existing stock of ideas; and thus we limit the conception. It is necessary therefore for the student to keep his mind fluid until he has had time to study the matter from various angles and to relate it to the many collateral subjects from which it is inseparable. If he fails to do this, he will find what will seem to be contradictions; that is, his studies will bring him to statements which do not agree with the too narrow ideas which he has already formed from his first incomplete study. The difficulty here is the same as is met with in any other study; statements which at first appear contradictory are later found to be merely supplementary.

Again, the term 'Astral Light' itself was borrowed from certain old philosophers, and has been borrowed many times by one writer or another, so that its meaning came to be vague and various; as those who used it were perhaps not very well informed, or each one used it in a sense of his own. Accordingly, when we read such a book as H. P. Blavatsky's *The Secret Doctrine,* we cannot safely assume that the term is always used in exactly the same sense, and shall need some judgment to decide in what sense it is being used at a given time. Sometimes other writers are referred to, such as Éliphas Lévi, and the word may be used in their sense. Sometimes we find it used as synonymous with Âkâśa, and sometimes as sharply distinguished therefrom. Such perplexities however will disappear on a more intimate study of *The Secret Doctrine,* and no doubt will be left as to the real meaning.

At the present time too we have the advantage of Dr. de Purucker's works, in which the teachings of *The Secret Doctrine* are so clearly analyzed; and it is now possible to give to the term 'astral light' a more precise meaning, which can be regarded as the accepted meaning. In *The Esoteric Tradition,* by G. de Purucker, pages 952 and following, we find a tabular arrangement of the principles of the universe, of which the following is a brief summary:

1. The Supreme Monad or Root, from which emanate the other principles, and called Paramâtman.
2. Alaya, Âkâśa, the origin of Cosmic Soul.
3. Mahat, or Cosmic Mind.
4. Cosmic Kâma, the desire or impelling force of the universe.
5. Cosmic Jîva or Vitality.
6. Astral Light; Cosmic Ether.
7. Sthûla-śarîra; the Physical Universe.

This then shows astral light as the next cosmic principle above the plane of our physical universe. It also shows astral light as the medium through which play the life-forces or 'lives,' collectively called cosmic Jîva, impelled as these are by cosmic desire. Finally, astral light is a medium connecting cosmic mind with the physical plane of nature. On pp. 949-50 of the same book we see the corresponding principles in the human constitution, the place of astral light being occupied by the linga-śarîra.

It is always important to remember that these various cosmic principles do not actually lie one above the other in layers, but are interblended. It is often necessary to represent them in a tabular form for purposes of explanation, but we must avoid letting that tabular form create a false picture in our mind. Physical science has made us familiar with the idea of different states of matter occupying the same space and interpenetrating one another; and this might be represented by a diagram in which they were placed one *above* another.

Furthermore, every septenary division in Nature is subdivided, and subdivided again, on the same septenary plan so that we can speak of various planes of the astral light and use such expressions as higher or lower astral light.

We find the following in G. de Purucker's *Occult Glossary*:

> The Astral Light is with regard to the material realms of the Solar System the copy or reflexion of what the Âkâśa is in the spiritual realms. The Astral Light is the mother of the physical, just as the Spirit is the mother of the Âkâśa or, inversely, the physical is merely the concretion of the astral, just as the Âkâśa is the veil or concretion of the highest Spiritual.—p. 21

APPENDIX

[The student may gain further insights into aspects of the Astral Light from the following extracts from the writings of H. P. Blavatsky and G. de Purucker.]

ASTRAL LIGHT.—The same as the *sidereal light* of Paracelsus and other Hermetic philosophers. Physically, it is the ether of modern science. Metaphysically, and in its spiritual, or occult sense, ether is a great deal more than is often imagined. In occult physics, and alchemy, it is well demonstrated to enclose within its shoreless waves not only Mr. Tyndall's *"promise* and potency of all terrestrial life," but also the *realization* of every quality of spirit. Alchemists and Hermetists believe that their astral, or sidereal ether, besides the above properties of sulphur, and white and red magnesia, or *magnes,* is the *anima mundi,* the workshop of Nature and of all the cosmos, spiritually, as well as physically. The "grand magisterium" asserts itself in the phenomenon of mesmerism, in the "levitation" of human and inert objects, and may be called the ether from its spiritual aspect.

The designation *astral* is ancient, and was used by some of the Neo-Platonists. Porphyry describes the celestial body which is always joined with the soul as "immortal, luminous, and starlike." The root of this word may be found, perhaps, in the Scythic *aist-aer*—which means star, or the Assyrian *Ishtar,* which, according to Burnouf has the same sense. As the Rosicrucians regarded the real as the direct opposite of the apparent, and taught that what seems light to *matter* is darkness to *spirit,* they searched for the latter in the astral ocean of invisible fire which encompasses the world; and claim to have traced the equally invisible spirit, which overshadows every man and is erroneously called *soul,* to the very throne of the Invisible and Unknown God. As the great cause must always remain invisible and imponderable, they could prove their assertions merely by demonstration of its effects in this world of matter, by calling them forth from the unknowable down into the knowable universe of effects. That this astral light permeates the whole cosmos, lurking in its latent state even in the minutest particle of rock, they demonstrate by the phenomenon of the spark from flint and from every other stone, whose spirit when forcibly disturbed springs to sight sparklike, and immediately disappears in the realms of the unknowable.

Paracelsus named it the *sidereal light,* taking the term from the Latin. He regarded the starry host (our earth included) as *condensed* portions of the astral light which "fell down into generation and matter," but whose magnetic or spiritual emanations kept constantly a never-ceasing intercommunication between themselves and the parent fount of all—the astral light. "The stars attract from us to themselves, and we from them again to us," he says. The body is wood and the life is fire, which comes like the light from the stars and from heaven. Everything pertaining to the spiritual world must come to us through the stars, and if we are in friendship with them, we may attain the greatest *magical* effects.

"As fire passes through an iron stove, so do the stars pass through man with all their properties and go into him as the rain into the earth, which gives fruit out of that same rain. Now observe that the stars *surround* the whole earth, *as a shell does the egg;* through the shell comes the air, and penetrates to the center of the world." The human body is subjected as well as the earth, and planets, and stars, to a double law; it attracts and repels, for it is saturated through with double magnetism, the influx of the astral light. Everything is double in nature; magnetism is positive and negative, active and passive, male and female. Night rests humanity from the day's activity, and restores the equilibrium of human as well as of cosmic nature. When the mesmerizer will have learned the grand secret of polarizing the action and endowing his fluid with a bisexual force he will have become the greatest magician living. Thus the astral light is androgyne, for equilibrium is the resultant of two opposing forces eternally reacting upon each other. The result of this is LIFE. *When the two forces are expanded and remain so long inactive, as to equal one another and so come to a complete rest, the condition* is DEATH. A human being can blow either a hot or a cold breath; and can absorb either cold or hot air. Every child knows how to regulate the temperature of his breath; but how to protect one's self from either hot or cold air, no physiologist has yet learned with certainty. The astral light alone, as the chief agent in magic, can discover to us all secrets of nature. The astral light is identical with the Hindu *âkâśa.*

—H. P. Blavatsky: *Isis Unveiled,* "Before the Veil," I, xxv-xxvi

The psychometer is clairvoyant; that is, he sees with the inner eye. Unless his will power is very strong, unless he has thoroughly trained himself to that particular phenomenon, and his knowledge of the capabilities of his sight are profound, his perceptions of places, persons, and events, must necessarily be very confused. But in the case of mesmerization, in which this same clairvoyant faculty is developed, the operator, whose will holds that of the subject under control, can force him to concentrate his attention upon a given picture long enough to observe all its minute details. Moreover, under the guidance of an experienced mesmerizer, the seer would excel the natural psychometer in having a prevision of future events, more distinct and clear than the latter. And to those who might object to the possibility of perceiving that which "yet is not," we may put the question: Why is it more impossible to see that which will be, than to bring back to sight that which is gone, and is no more? According to the kabalistic doctrine, the future exists in the astral light in embryo, as the present existed in embryo in the past. While man is free to act as he pleases, the manner in which he *will* act was foreknown from all time; not on the ground of fatalism or destiny, but simply on the principle of universal, unchangeable harmony; and, as it may be foreknown that when a musical note is struck, its vibrations will not, and cannot change into those of another note. Besides, eternity can have neither past nor future, but only the present; as boundless space, in its strictly literal sense, can have neither distant nor proximate places. Our conceptions, limited to the narrow area of our experience, attempt to fit if not an end, at least a beginning of time and space; but neither of these exist in reality; for in such case time would not be eternal, nor space boundless. The past no more exists than the future, as we have said, only our memories survive; and our memories are but the glimpses that we catch of the reflections of this past in the currents of the astral light, as the psychometer catches them from the astral emanations of the object held by him.

—*Op. cit.*, I, 184

There are two kinds of magnetization; the first is purely *animal*, the other transcendent, and depending on the will and knowledge of the mesmerizer, as well as on the degree of spirituality of the subject, and his capacity to receive the impressions of the astral light. And here it may be observed that clairvoyance depends a great deal more on the former than on the latter. To the power of an adept, like Du Potet, the most *positive* subject will have to submit. If his sight is ably directed by the mesmerizer, magician, or spirit, the light must yield up its most secret records to our scrutiny; for, if it is a book which is ever closed to those "who see and do not perceive," on the other hand it is ever opened for one who *wills* to see it opened. It keeps an unmutilated record of all that was, that is, or ever will be. The minutest acts of our lives are imprinted on it, and even our thoughts rest photographed on its eternal tablets. It is the book which we see opened by the angel in the *Revelation,* "which is the Book of life, and out of which the dead are judged according to their works." It is, in short, the MEMORY of GOD!"

—*Op. cit.,* I, 178

In her *Reminiscences of H. P. Blavatsky and "The Secret Doctrine"* (p. 33), Countess Wachtmeister relates how she once asked H.P.B. "how it was that she could make mistakes in setting down what was given to her." H.P.B. answered as follows:

"Well, you see, what I do is this. I make what I can only describe as a sort of vacuum in the air before me, and mix my sight and my will upon it, and soon scene after scene passes before me like the successive pictures of a diorama, or, if I need a reference or information from some book, I fix my mind intently, and the astral counterpart of the book appears, and from it I take what I need. The more perfectly my mind is freed from distractions and mortifications, the more energy and intentness it possesses, the more easily I can do this; but today, after all the vexations I have undergone in consequence of the letter from X., I could not concentrate properly, and each time I tried I got the quotations all wrong. . . ."

—Compiler's footnote in *Blavatsky: Collected Writings*, VI, 151

(This footnote was appended by H.P.B. to that portion of her sister's narrative, used by A. P. Sinnett in his text, that described the manner in which the genealogy of H.P.B.'s family was reconstructed with the help of occult methods. Sinnett says: "This lasted for months. Never during that time were Mme. Blavatsky's invisible helper or helpers found mistaken in any single instance." To this H.P.B. remarks:)

Indeed not; for it was neither a "spirit" nor "spirits" but living men who can draw before their eyes the picture of any book or manuscript wherever existing, and in case of need that of any long forgotten and unrecorded event, who helped "Mme. Blavatsky." The astral light is the store-house and the record book of all things, and deeds have no secrets for such men. And the proof of it may be found in the production of *Isis Unveiled.*

—*Blavatsky*: *Collected Writings,* VII, 250 (printed under the title "Miscellaneous Notes," from *Incidents in the Life of Madame Blavatsky,* by A. P. Sinnett)

It is customary among many people, either from thoughtlessness or from ignorance, to speak of the Astral World or Realm as being separated off from the physical world by a 'partition,' or by some similar dividing element, which supposedly, according to this totally erroneous idea, thus prevents, or is a bar to, free and easy intercourse or interchange between the astral and physical worlds respectively. Nothing could be farther from the truth than this totally wrong conception. One might almost exclaim, "Would that it were so!"

There is absolutely no such partition or barrier or wall between the physical and the astral, for they in very truth melt into or blend with each other by indistinguishable gradations of matter verging from the most ethereal-physical into the most astral-material. There is, therefore, constant, uninterrupted, and incesant interchange between the physical and the astral world; and the only 'partition' or barrier that actually exists is those few grades of blending substances, which, far from being obstacles or obstructions to intercourse, actually and in very truth are the means of communication — somewhat as the electric wire is the medium for communicating the electric current from point to point.

There are times in human history, which recur with cyclic or periodic regularity, when these few intervening 'grades' between the physical and the astral seem to wear thin; and at such times there occurs an inevitable and inescapable outbreak of psycho-astral happenings in the physical world and in human society, due to the 'thinness' of the 'grades' just spoken of. We are at the present time in just such a state of astral-psychical outcroppings. These periods are invariably attended with very real dangers or perils both to human mentality and emotional stability, although they have the one redeeming feature— if indeed it may be called such—of arousing men's interest in things other than physical, and of suggesting to their minds the actual existence of spheres or worlds of being more ethereal than the physical.

The lesson to learn, however, is that these more ethereal worlds, are by no means or necessarily more *spiritual* than the physical; for the physical sphere is a highly safe and sane place, when compared with the lower regions of the astral world, as above stated, with which intercourse from the physical plane is most easily established.

—G. de Purucker: *The Esoteric Tradition,* II, 779-80, footnote

. . . After the physical body has been cast off and the Reimbodying Ego is freed from the attractions of the physical sphere, it remains for a certain time in the lower planes or realms of the Astral Light, and finally there occurs the 'second death' which means that the Reimbodying Ego there and then casts off or drops the kâma-rûpa —the more or less exact duplication in form or appearance of the man as he was when alive on Earth. Thus it is that the lower realms of the Astral Light are literally filled with multitudes of such kâma-rûpas or forms or shapes, each one a more or less perfect duplication of the previously living being or entity as it was on Earth.

It is these kâma-rûpas, or astral *reliquiae* which are the *simulacra* or astral likenesses of the beings who had lived on Earth, who are the 'spooks' or *eidola* spoken of in the Esoteric Philosophy. They are all soulless, i.e., mere 'shells,' because the Reimbodying Ego, which had formerly used its astral kâma-rûpa as its intermediary between itself and the physical body, now is free from its kâma-rûpa, and is on its peregrinations towards the Devachan.

When these kâma-rûpas or astral spooks are of extremely evil and grossly-living men on Earth, they then form what are called Elementaries, still containing some remnant of personal intelligence and still filled with the astral automatic instincts, and hence are very dangerous creatures—being entities of evil passions and tendencies—for living human beings to attempt to associate with through mediums or otherwise.

—*Op. cit.*, II, 761, footnote

MANUALS IN THIS SERIES

1. THEOSOPHY: A General View of Occult Doctrine —*C. J. Ryan*
2. REINCARNATION: A Lost Chord in Modern Thought —*L. L. Wright*
3. THE DOCTRINE OF KARMA: Chance or Justice? —*G. van Pelt, M.D.*
4. MAN AND HIS SEVEN PRINCIPLES: An Ancient Basis for a New Psychology —*L. L. Wright*
5. AFTER DEATH — WHAT? —*L. L. Wright*
6. EVOLUTION: Who and What is Man? —*H. T. Edge*
7. MAN'S DIVINE PARENTAGE AND DESTINY: The Great Rounds and Races —*G. van Pelt, M.D.*
8. CYCLES: In Universe and Man —*Lydia Ross, M.D.*
9. HIERARCHIES: The Cosmic Ladder of Life —*G. van Pelt, M.D.*
10. THE ASTRAL LIGHT: Nature's Amazing Picture Gallery —*H. T. Edge*
11. PSYCHIC POWERS —*Helen Todd*
12. THEOSOPHY AND CHRISTIANITY —*H. T. Edge*